Assisted Living:
Questions I Wish I Had Asked

By Marcy Baskin

What You Need To Know Before You Decide

©2013 ElderRoads Publishing

ISBN-13: 978-0615881003 (Custom Universal)
ISBN-10: 0615881009

*"There is beauty to be found in the changing
of the earth's seasons,
and an inner grace in honouring the cycles
of life"*

-Jack Kornfeld

Gratitude

With loving thanks and appreciation to:

My amazing husband Steven, my forever best friend, and staunch supporter, for inspiring me and lifting me up more times than I can count

My sister Lori, editor and sibling extraordinaire, for walking next to me on the road of our parents' illnesses, holding my hand, and never wavering

Bobby and Buddy Saltzman, my dear parents, their unconditional love and limitless faith in me continues to inspire me even in their earthly absence

Jodi Gold and Helene Roos, two of the best executive coaches (and friends) on the planet

Pam, Henrietta, Laura, Lanny, Phil, Geri, Anne, Becky and all the other amazing people I met on this journey – for sharing their stories with me and holding me when I needed it

Villa Capri at Varenna, my mother's home for the last three years of her life, for their patience during my distress and more important, for the great care my mother received while living there

The Alzheimer's Association, for their tireless dedication to finding a cure and for creating a container to hold and support all of us affected by this relentless disease.

A portion of the proceeds from sales of this book will be donated to the Alzheimer's Association

CONTENTS

Inspiration

It came as no surprise when my mother was diagnosed with early stage Alzheimer's Disease. We had been noticing her forgetfulness, her decreasing ability to perform tasks that were once easy, and the confusion that started to plague her on a regular basis. For awhile we held on to hope for another explanation for these troubling symptoms. We wondered for a time, could it be the fifteen years of caregiving for my father, the loss of her dream of an active retirement, and living so far from her family? Depression? A urinary tract infection? One can only mistake dementia for something else for so long. After awhile, my sister and I could no longer deny that Mom was ill and she needed our help.

Some families care for their elders at home until the end of life. In our case, we had parents who were firm in their resolve never to move in with their children. When my father passed away, Mom wanted her own place to live. Even when we offered her a room and bath of her own in our home, she was adamant about her need for independence.

We tried round-the-clock care for her at her apartment, but she felt lonely and isolated. I visited nearly every day but visits from your daughter, while appreciated, don't fill the need for friends and peers.

We began our search for the right situation. Mom was at a stage where what she needed most was light supervision, meal preparation, and reminders to take her medications. She was socially engaged and didn't need help with most daily tasks. Independent living was not enough supervision, memory care was too much. An assisted living community seemed to be the right balance of independence and support when she needed it.

We visited communities and small care homes, narrowed it down to a few, and chose the one that appeared to be a good fit; it was clean, cheerful, active, and beautifully decorated. We sat down with management, and covered what we thought was an in-depth list of important questions. We felt we had made a good choice and that it would be smooth sailing once Mom moved in. The challenges over the next three years revealed that we had not, in fact, been thorough in finding out what to expect from assisted living. How could we know? We had never done this before!

Our mother's deterioration was painful, for her and for us. I understand now that although I couldn't have changed the course of my mother's illness, I could have better prepared myself for this unfamiliar territory -- by making sure I understood exactly how this thing called assisted living would work.

How do you prepare accurate financial projections for when care needs increase? How high is the staff turnover rate? How will I be informed about changes in medication and would I be asked for my input? How often would Mom be re-assessed for care needs? What if there is an emergency and I am out of town? What medical care is offered? Not knowing these (and other) details made an emotionally taxing journey even harder to navigate.

In hindsight, spending precious time with my mother that was not task-oriented or that did not feel like I was always putting out fires, would have been a more fulfilling way for us to spend our final days together.

So I offer you this: one part of your toolkit for moving through the tricky waters that lie ahead. Use it not only to get the answers to the questions I've offered, but also to stimulate your own fact-finding process. Knowing what to look for will help you manage your expectations, and do your very best to create a collaborative relationship with those who are providing care for your loved one on a daily basis.

Take a deep breath. Appreciate yourself for choosing to be there for your loved one when she or he needs it the most. Your efforts, kindness, and compassion matter!

HOW TO USE THIS BOOK

Smile, breathe and go slowly.

– Thich Nhat Hanh

This book is offered in service to the task you are facing -- to help you make sense of the process of choosing an assisted living or memory care community. It is not a guide to making the decision that precedes a move into a senior care facility. Each person's preferences, family, and care plan are different and should be geared to providing the best quality of life possible. For some, care at home works best. For others, a group situation is a better fit. Many people will enjoy a lively, active environment – others prefer quiet and less commotion. If you have chosen (or are thinking about choosing) a residential care option, then you'll find these questions to be comprehensive, detailed, and hopefully, a huge help during your search and in ultimately making a good choice. Engaging a placement specialist in your area can be extremely helpful, as they know the ins and outs of the different options. Most placement specialists are paid a referral fee by the community and do not charge the family anything.

There can be misconceptions about what you can realistically expect from assisted living. You should know right at the get-go that this is a *non-medical* option. Instead of going into detail here about this, I suggest you become familiar with any and all medical needs of your loved one and discuss them when you interview a facility.

Although it may be hard to think about, stay open to the idea that things will change and usually progress in terms of needs. Even harder would be to subject your loved one (and yourself) to another move down the road.

This is a complex assignment you have taken on. It will require patience, diligence, and a lot of reading between the lines for you to assemble information, compare different options, and figure out which place will best serve the needs of your loved one. On page 17 you will find a form you can use to organize the basic factual data for each facility. On my website you can download a copy of this, as well as a worksheet to take with you on appointments. Here is the link:

www.elderroads.com/my-book.html

Note the tips and a variety of things to consider, in *grey* in each section. You'll also find a glossary and a list of helpful resources at the back of the book.

This is probably a new and unknown world to you. There are over 200 questions presented here and you absolutely do not need to read or use all of them. You may feel somewhat overwhelmed and see this as a nearly impossible amount of information to gather and digest. There are no hard and fast "right" answers to many of the questions. Take some time to think about what matters most to your loved one and to you. The questions (and answers) that apply will emerge.

As the quote at the beginning of this section suggests, at the very least try to breathe and go slowly. It may be hard to smile in the beginning but as you start to gain confidence in your ability to filter through the mountain of information coming your way, a part of you will relax into the knowledge that you are doing your very best.

Although the title might imply that the questions apply solely to one type of senior care community, the majority of them are germane to assisted living, small care homes (board and care), memory care, and some of the issues raised are relevant to skilled nursing facilities, as well. Skilled nursing facilities are strictly regulated compared to the lesser degree of oversight and compliance requirements at the assisted living level. An interesting fact is that the way the terminology defines care levels today, assisted living includes board and care as well as memory care. Remember.....anything under the auspices of assisted living is a *non-medical* model.

You may notice references to various stages of cognitive impairment and/or dementia; however, even if you are transitioning a loved one who is still mentally competent but simply needs a little assistance and a few reminders, you will be well-served by this assortment of questions.

A more than ample guide, this book will help you think of questions of your own – I have left blank areas throughout for you to record your thoughts and questions. There is no doubt that you will have many as you proceed.

Should you find yourself stuck or overwhelmed to the point where you are not moving forward, you can also contact me. I can work on the phone or via Skype if you are not within a comfortable driving distance to the San Francisco Bay Area. Sometimes it takes an outsider to help get the process in motion, facilitate uncomfortable conversations, and to provide a less emotional, more objective perspective.

Take a deep breath. Exhale.
You can do this.

RESIDENCE INFORMATION

Name_____

Address_____

Date/Time of visit_____

Contact
Person_____

Owner (if different)_____

Phone_____Email_____

Website?_____

RCFE# (assisted living)_____

How long in operation?_____

Other facilities owned, past and current

_____

_____

References*_____

_____

_____

Type of Community

__Independent   __ Assisted Living
__Board and Care   __Memory Care
__Skilled Nursing   __Other

In addition to assisted living services, this community also offers:

__Dementia Care   __Hospice/End-
                                   of-Life Care

Have any complaints been filed about this community? (Check with the local Ombudsman, Council on Aging, County Office, Public Health Department, Community Care Licensing, etc. for complaints and if/how they were resolved)_____

_____

_____

Insurance Accepted?_____(Y/N)

If yes, what types of insurance are accepted and what is expected coverage?

One of the most informative and helpful references is a current resident and/or a family member

---

Management Team:

ExecutiveDirector_____

Operations _____

Maintenance_____

Marketing_____

Medical_____

Activities_____

Food Services_____

Business/Financial_____

Other_____

YOUR VISIT

It is a good idea to plan more than one visit. There is a different feel to active, "primetime" hours than during the quiet times, and weekdays vs. weekends – remember, your loved one will be living there 24/7. Have a meal, participate in an activity with your loved one, meet/talk to other residents, their family members, and staff. Visit after dinner or around bedtime. The people who work at night often have less supervision than the day staff. Sometimes they have more responsibility due to a higher resident-to- caregiver ratio. A good idea might be to show up after dinner and observe: are the caregivers on duty checking on sleeping residents and engaging with those who are awake? Or are they sitting in a group passing time, reading magazines, or texting? What are the residents doing after dinner? Holidays and weekends are also a good time to visit for a different perspective.

Observe and take note of the following:

Cleanliness of public areas including restrooms, activity rooms, dining areas, library, etc.

Cleanliness and equipment in kitchen facilities

What are the residents doing during your visit?

Is there a group activity going on? Do the people participating seem reasonably engaged?

Notice interactions between staff and residents, what do you see and hear?

Do staff members appear to be warm, and respectful? Are they making eye contact with the resident to whom they are speaking?

If there is music playing, is it too loud for people who are not hearing impaired or too soft for those who are? What kind of music is it?

Is there anyone sitting alone in a wheelchair facing a wall?

Are there any unpleasant odors?

When there is an unpleasant odor in a public space, often caused by "accidents", how is it dealt with?

Knowing what you do about your loved one, can you envision her or him living in this facility?

Imagine yourself visiting. What it would feel like? Is the environment depressing or reasonably cheerful? Would you eat the food that is served in the dining room?

YOUR VISIT cont'd

View both an empty room and a room that is currently rented. The empty room can show you the general condition and any deferred maintenance. A room that is in use (preferred to one that is staged or used as a model) will give you a sense of how well the housekeeping staff maintains the space and what the room will be like when occupied. Notice the lighting, the view from the windows, and even the acoustics.

Where will the bed go? How many personal belongings will fit into the space and what will you do with the things that won't? Identify items you know will be most important and be sure that they can come along.

Bring a pad and pen, an iPad, this book, or the worksheet to keep track of questions that you may think of while you are on your tour (or afterwards). You probably won't remember them all if you don't make a list. When you visit a place of interest for the second time, bring a tape measure and if possible, the dimensions of any furniture you plan to move to the apartment or room.

If you have any questions about cleanliness and sanitary conditions, you can ask to see a copy of a recent state inspection. This should be made available to you if requested.

Some residences place a lot of emphasis on a beautiful lobby, fresh flowers, etc. These are nice touches but it is important to dig much deeper.....Be sure to check with Long Term Care Ombudsmen or other state agencies regarding citations, complaints, licensing issues, and how/if these were resolved.

_____

_____

_____

_____

_____

_____

_____

_____

_____

ACCOMMODATIONS, AMENITIES, AND COST

What options does the community offer – studio, 1 bedroom, 2 bedroom, etc.? Are shared rooms available at a reduced cost?

Are there accommodations for couples?

How much is the base rent and what is included? (You might ask what is *not* included)

How are care costs calculated? What is the average care cost?

How much have rent and care costs increased over the last five years?

This is very important – even if your loved one does not require much care at the time he moves into the residence, things can change. It is reasonable for you to ask to see a copy of the guidelines they use to assess care costs. It is not something that is routinely offered to family members but they will usually let you review this information if you ask. You have a right to know how charges will be assessed (see section on Care for more on this)

The cost for care can be very high, depending on what a person needs. Many of us don't consider the almost certain increase in monthly expense as time goes on.

Is there a pleasant outside space where residents spend time in good weather?

During your visits, notice how many residents are outside.

Cleaning/Linens/Personal Laundry – how often are these done and what is the charge if a resident wants an extra cleaning or load of laundry?

Are overnight visitors (family) permitted? Is there a charge?

Is personal transportation offered for doctor appointments, shopping, errands? How often is it available and what is the cost?

What are the limitations of the transportation service (distance, days, times, destinations)?

What type of personal emergency call system is in place (such as Lifeline bracelets or pendants, or other)?

Where are the call buttons located in the apartment and if activated by a resident, who gets the call?

ACCOMMODATIONS, AMENITIES AND COST cont'd

Is there a low-income program? How many units are reserved for low-income? What qualifies as low-income?

If you think you may qualify for a low-income program, ask for more details. It is an entire application process in itself and usually takes some time to get approval. The Marketing Director will have this information or you will be referred to the Business Manager.

If a resident moves from one unit to another within the community (for example, from Assisted Living to Memory Care or to simply downsize their living space), what is the approximate cost of the move, if any?

Is there an entrance fee (sometimes called a community fee)? Is it negotiable?

What happens if a resident runs out of money?

There are things that may be negotiable and others that are not. Rent may or may not be negotiable. It would be unusual for care fees to be negotiated. If there is an entrance fee or buy-in of some sort, you would be well within reason to ask about getting it reduced. This is more common in higher end residences and sometimes the Marketing Director is prepared to lower this fee. Sometimes she cannot. Make sure you are clear and feel comfortable with how much will be refunded if the situation does not work out for your family and you decide to leave after 30, 60, or 90 days. <u>Get this in writing</u>!

THE RESIDENTS

How many residents?

What is the average age of residents?

How many men?___women?___couples?___

Is this a historically typical ratio?

General level of cognitive function of current residents?

Cultural demographics of current residents (ethnic, nationality, religious, etc.)

Is there a forum or resident council that meets regularly with management? Can families attend?

Who leads the resident council? Ask to meet that person. Ask about past issues and how they were resolved.

Are pets permitted to live at this residence? Is there an additional cost?

If a new resident has trouble adjusting, what support is offered?

Is a prospective resident required to be ambulatory to move into the community?

Has a resident ever been asked to leave? What were the circumstances?

How does the facility handle romantic relationships and/or consensual sex between residents?

Your expectations regarding "engagement"

If your loved one is a person who has always preferred to spend a lot of time alone, try to be realistic in your expectations of how he will interact with other residents in the community. You do want to be sure that there are options for contact and that socializing is encouraged and facilitated. If your person is already somewhat reserved or even uncommunicative, you shouldn't expect that living in a community would necessarily change that.

_____

_____

_____

_____

_____

_____

_____

STAFF

You can learn a lot simply by paying attention and observing the caregivers at work. Consider that these employees are often paid very low wages and have a lot of pressure placed upon them. Do they appear to be kind, patient, and respectful, or distracted, harried, insensitive? Their task is not an easy one; that said, part of their job is to keep any dissatisfaction with their work circumstances to themselves and their supervisors, and to remain outwardly calm, friendly, and attentive to the needs of the residents. Meet with the person who supervises the caregivers and ask about what kinds of problems arise and how they are handled. Also ask who is the back up person when the supervisor is not in the building.

What is the caregiver to resident ratio?

Are there caregivers who stay awake all night? This is always the case in larger assisted living residences, in memory care and skilled nursing; however, if you are considering a smaller care home, this is an important question to ask.

What are the minimum qualifications an applicant needs in order to be hired as a caregiver in this facility?

Are background checks, fingerprinting, integrity tests given to potential new hires? Any other screenings?

Describe the training given to new caregivers

What kind of ongoing training, if any, is offered/required for caregivers?

Are caregivers and other staff given specific training in caring for someone with dementia?

Are there incentives for caregivers who demonstrate extraordinary job performance or participate in additional training?

What are the caregivers' responsibilities? What would be considered out of their scope of work?

What is the rate of turnover? Length of employment of current staff?

If there seems to be a high turnover, ask why.

Do caregivers speak the same language as your loved one?

If the community has different levels of care (assisted living, memory care), is the training different for each level? What are the key differences?

Are caregivers designated to a particular area or are they moved around?

STAFF cont'd

> *Consistency is comforting and can create a familial feeling and camaraderie for residents. Seeing the same caregivers repeatedly can reduce anxiety, especially for people with dementia. Even if a person doesn't know a caregiver's name, she probably knows when she is looking at a familiar face. Familiarity with the residents is important, too, as caregivers get to know their preferences and idiosyncrasies. The overall experience of a resident can be more positive by forming these relationships.*

What is the policy regarding families hiring outside caregivers?

When are managers on duty?

How many caregivers are working on the weekends?

Is the weekend staffing level different than during the week?

Have there been any issues with theft of residents' possessions? Ask for details in terms of how often this has occurred and if/how the situation was resolved.

What prior experience must a potential manager have in order to be considered?

Is there a manager on site on weekends? If not, who is in charge?

Ask to meet the Executive Director (the person in charge of the entire residence).

_____

_____

_____

_____

_____

_____

_____

_____

_____

_____

CARE

Care Needs Assessment

How is an assessment for the level of care required conducted before moving into the facility?

Who performs the assessments?

How often are residents re-assessed for care needs?

Are families involved or are they contacted after a re-assessment has been conducted?

What are the criteria to determine if a resident's care needs exceed what is available at the assisted living level? (*This is very important, both for present and expected future needs*)

How is a move to a memory care unit decided upon and handled (assuming this option is available)?

Can residents of assisted living participate in a "day program" in memory care as a way to begin the transition?

Does the facility offer any kind of day program to help transition a new resident from home to assisted living or memory care?

Is respite care available? What is the cost?

Activities of Daily Living (ADL)

Incontinence Care

How often is an incontinent resident toileted? Is it on a regular schedule or as needed or both?

How often are incontinent residents checked?

Who provides incontinence supplies?

If the community provides supplies, what is the cost?

Consider buying your own supplies and delivering them when you visit. It might be worth it to you if you think the mark up added is too high. Highly personal tip: Spot check to be sure that the caregivers are using the right size, especially if they are supplying the diapers, or even if you are supplying them. For obvious reasons, it can be an undignified and uncomfortable situation for your loved one if the wrong size is used.

Bathing/Grooming

How often are residents bathed/showered?

Hair washed?

How much time is allotted in the caregiver's schedule to attend to bathing?

CARE cont'd

What strategies are used if a resident refuses to be bathed?

What is meant by grooming, at this particular care home?

<u>Dressing</u>

Many residents are able to dress themselves, even in early and middle stages of dementia. They should be encouraged to do so for as long as possible, perhaps with a caregiver standing by if they need assistance. Some communities have creative ways of organizing a resident's closet if they are beginning to have trouble choosing proper clothing. Ask about this.

If your loved one soils his shirt during a meal, will he be reminded or taken to put on a clean shirt? This is a dignity, not safety or healthcare issue, but so important.

If your loved one resists getting dressed, how is that handled?

Some people are simply not "morning people" and prefer not to dress, shower, or go to breakfast, at an early hour. How is that accommodated?

If you choose to hire a private caregiver, what is this person permitted to do as far as care and ADLs?

In the case of a couple, is the capable spouse allowed to provide care functions (medication management, dressing, bathing, etc.)? If so, are they charged for it anyway?

Ambulation

How is a non-ambulatory person handled and what are the costs involved?

In memory care, how often are residents taken outdoors?

Are two person lifts or transfers available?

Does the community use a Hoyer lift (*see* glossary)? Are all caregivers trained in how to use it?

_____

_____

_____

_____

_____

CARE cont'd

> *Even if your loved one can walk on her own, it is possible that at some point, that may change. It is important to know what accommodation will be made for residents who require a "two-person transfer" or the use of a lift. Ask to see the lift but be prepared that you may find it rather disturbing. You might ask someone to use it on you so that you know what it feels like to be transferred in this way. I did that and although it was not painful, it was quite unsettling. Ask about what kind of training is provided for caregivers in using a mechanical lift, both for use of the equipment and for maintaining dignity.*

<u>Other questions</u>

Is medical staff available on weekends?

What is the policy when staff notices a change in condition that in their opinion, might require further attention or adjustment in care? Do they call the physician directly? Is the family notified first?

If necessary, can simple wound care (changing dressing) be provided at the resident's room or apartment?

You can absolutely request to be the first point of contact in a "change in condition" assessment, when there is an apparent change in behavior, cognition, or physical symptoms. Be extra vigilant if/when the staff suggests that your loved one needs anti-anxiety or anti-psychotic medication. If it is presented to you that your family member is "combative", request a specific description of the behaviors that led to that assessment and verify it with other caregivers.

"Uncooperative" behavior can be inconvenient for staff, especially when they are caring for many residents, but is not necessarily combative, requiring pharmaceutical intervention. Sometimes a person with dementia cannot communicate simple needs such as "I'm cold or hungry or thirsty or have a full bladder" and acts out because their needs are not understood or being met. This can be a signal of frustration and unhappiness, rather than combative behavior. If the behavior can be traced to a basic need, future interactions with the resident will be informed and the behavior might well shift. This is one of the reasons why proper training is essential in dementia care.

CARE cont'd

> *You can and should expect to be notified if there is any change in medication. Even if you have an "agreement" with the physician's office to be contacted, it may not be reliable. The nurse at the residence should contact you before any change in medication or dosage is implemented.*

Are there motion sensors in resident rooms?

Are the motion sensors activated all the time or only at night? If your loved one takes a nap during the day, how will the staff know if she is awake and needs assistance? This is assuming that she is unable to either get out of bed on her own or call for assistance.

Are there volunteers working at the community?

How are they screened, who supervises them and what do they do?

_____

_____

_____

_____

_____

_____

_____

_____

_____

_____

_____

_____

_____

_____

MEDICAL SERVICES and MEDICATION MANAGEMENT

Is there a doctor available on-site or on call at the community? How often?

Is there a full time nurse available on-site? What days and hours?

How does the staff keep track of residents' medical records (Electronic? Paper files?)

Who has access to medical records?

Do residents receive preventive care such as flu shots, pneumonia shots?

Are staff members required to get flu shots?

As people age, they often take multiple medications, which can become a complex process. It requires impeccable systems of communication between doctors, nurses, pharmacies, med tecs, caregivers, and family.

What are the qualifications and training for the med managers (sometimes called med tecs)?

How many different med managers are there and how do they communicate with one another?

Who will order prescription refills (you or someone at the community)?

Does the care home work with a particular pharmacy to fill prescriptions?

Does that pharmacy research drug interactions when prescriptions are submitted?

If a change in medication order is received directly from the physician, what is the protocol for notifying the family? (Preferably it would be before the prescription is filled or administered).

What is the community's track record regarding medication errors? To whom is that reported? Is that record available to the public?

If the family is providing the meds, a last minute phone call or email advising that the resident is "on their last pill" and more meds are required within 24 hours doesn't work. What that means to you is that no matter where you are or what you are doing, refilling this prescription (or over the counter item) goes to the top of your to-do list. It is reasonable to expect that the people who dispense and regulate medication have the ability to notice and report when supply is running low. This may seem ridiculously obvious; assume nothing and ask the question. I experienced many-a-frantic last minute phone calls to the pharmacy when informed that my mother had just taken her last dose of something important – blood thinner, anti-depressant, etc.

ACTIVITIES

A skilled and dedicated activity director can make all the difference in the level of enjoyment and stimulation experienced by residents. Even when my mother was in a wheel chair, couldn't speak or read, the Activity Director would wheel her to the activity (which was usually a word game, drawing, painting, musical performance) and keep her in the room, seated right next to her. My mother always had a smile on her face during these times.

Who supervises and who facilitates activities for residents?

What are their backgrounds and qualifications?

How many hours per week is this person at the community, conducting activities for residents?

Who facilitates activities when the Activity Director is not there?

What does a typical day look like?

Is there a dedicated activity director for Assisted Living and Memory Care or is it the same person for both? (It is better if they are dedicated – it's a big job and needs are different for each population)

Does she/he have other responsibilities? What are they?

Request to meet this person.

How many people, on average, attend the activities that will likely be of interest to your loved one?

How often are activities cancelled?

Do residents in Memory Care attend appropriate events with Assisted Living residents? If yes, which ones?

Describe types and frequency of activities:

Daily? Weekends?

Music, Pet Therapy, Off-site trips, exercise classes, art classes, book club, discussion groups, etc.

How many drivers are on staff?

What happens to scheduled transportation and off site activities if the driver calls in sick?

Here's why this is important: If there is no designated back up, residents who need personal or group transportation are stranded – unless another licensed person steps in, leaving their other responsibilities unattended

EMERGENCY PROCEDURES

What types of occurrences are automatically deemed an emergency (calling 911)?

Who determines if an ER visit is required?

Is the family contacted before calling EMTs?

> *If someone is bleeding, having trouble breathing, or is unconscious, you cannot expect to be called before emergency personnel is contacted. That said, if a situation falls within the community's definition of an emergency but is not life threatening, you can ask to be the first point of contact (dizziness, unusual confusion, etc.)*

Who has access to your contact information and where is it located?

Can any caregiver or employee access your contact information electronically? Or is there a central hard copy somewhere in the building that will need to be located in order to find the best way to get in touch with you? This can be very important during an emergency.

Who will accompany your family member to the ER if you are not available? Will they charge you for this?

What systems are in place to honor wishes outlined in an Advance Directive, POLST form, or DNR? Have there been any past issues?

If your loved one has an Advance Directive, POLST form, or DNR, copies need to be on file as well as in the apartment or room where she lives. You should have a copy, too. Most emergency personnel are trained to take a quick look on a refrigerator door or some other obvious place for these documents.

It goes without saying that you would not want your loved one to be alone during a trip to the ER. It is usually a liability issue that requires the community to send someone; know the policy so you know what to expect should this come up. Not knowing in advance will only create more stress for you at what is an already high alert moment. If you are notified promptly of a situation, you (or a trusted friend or family member) can possibly be at the ER when the ambulance arrives. Also discuss how this would be handled if you are out of town and if there are any forms to fill out for a friend, relative, or geriatric care manager to be your stand-in should there be an emergency.

How is a quarantine handled when multiple residents are suffering from a flu or other contagious conditions?

During a quarantine, what <u>additional</u> precautions are taken in daily care protocols (use of gloves, masks, meals served in-room, limiting visitors, etc)?

EMERGENCY PROCEDURES cont'd

What are some examples of medical situations that can be handled by the staff?

What would be considered out of a caregiver's scope of work?

What is the protocol if a resident falls?
Are caregivers permitted to lift someone who has fallen? Do they have training to do this?

What
 type of personal alarm systems are used and where are they located (in the bathroom, next to the bed, bracelet or pendant, other)?

What is the average response time when a personal alarm system is activated by a resident (or family member)?

Have there been any complaints concerning response time?

> *A person suffering from dementia will likely not remember how to use a personal call system or even know what it is!*

What is the procedure in case of fire?

How often does the staff participate in fire drills or emergency training?

What systems are in place in case of a power outage?

If the building needs to be evacuated, what procedures are in place?

_____

_____

_____

_____

_____

_____

_____

_____

_____

_____

_____

_____

FOOD

Chances are, your loved one will be transitioning from having her own kitchen and refrigerator, stocked with the foods she likes and is accustomed to eating at the times she prefers, to having meals prepared by someone else and eaten as a group at specified times. It's important to understand how decisions are made about what will be served and how various preferences and needs are addressed. Meals are often the most consistent social interaction people have when they are reside in an assisted living environment. The dining room should be pleasant, immaculate, well-lit, preferably with many windows, and have good accessibility for people with walkers and wheelchairs. Notice how the dining room smells – are the aromas tempting? Ask about how residents who may be reluctant to go to the dining room are encouraged to do so. Ask a resident how he likes the food!

Are there specific meal times or can a resident come to the dining room at any time during the day and be served?

If the meal times are at specified hours, what are they?

If a resident misses a meal due to an appointment, a nap, or other circumstance, can they come to the dining area or kitchen and request something simple like a sandwich or bowl of soup?

Are healthy snacks available during the day?

Are residents offered a menu, for those who are able to make food choices? Ask for a copy of this week's menu. Have a meal if time allows.

Are fresh fruits and vegetables offered at every meal?

What are the general dietary guidelines followed (are salt, sugar, and fat content monitored)?

How do you ensure that meals meet high nutritional standards?

Who creates the menus and what are their credentials?

How are special dietary considerations accommodated, e.g. vegetarian, Kosher, diabetic, food allergies?

How is meal attendance tracked? How do you know if someone has actually eaten or not eaten at mealtime?

How do you track residents who are losing/gaining weight?

Are meals served in rooms if requested? Is there an extra charge?

WHAT ELSE CAN MY FAMILY EXPECT?

Who is your contact person and how accessible are they if you have questions? And you will have many, particularly in the beginning.

What are the most common complaints at this facility?

What is the procedure if a family has a complaint and how are complaints handled?

Are there regular updates for families?

You might consider asking about a particularly difficult conflict with a resident's family and how it was resolved.

Has a resident ever been asked to leave? Why?

Are there events/activities that include family participation?

What is usually done for the big holidays? (Thanksgiving, Chanukah, Christmas, etc.)

Is there a support group offered for families? How often? Is it free of charge?

> *Try a support group – even if you feel that you aren't a "group person". It can be a source of great comfort. A good place to start to look for a group is the Alzheimer's Association (www.alz.org)*

CHECKLIST OF MISCELLANEOUS SERVICES
(and cost, if any)

☐ Podiatry

☐ Dental

☐ Flu/Pneumonia Vaccination Clinic

☐ Audiology testing

☐ Voting/Polling place

☐ Physical Therapy

☐ Computers for residents' or family use

☐ WiFi

☐ Hair Salon

☐ Religious Services

☐ Massage

☐ Other

_____

_____

_____

_____

_____

_____

_____

_____

_____

_____

_____

_____

_____

_____

A Few Final Words

Now that you have read these questions, perhaps you have started to feel overwhelmed by what may seem to be undignified and unthinkable circumstances. Let me leave you with a few thoughts of a different nature.

In the end, your choice to fully take on the well-being of someone else is the most beautiful gift you may ever give in your life. There is an authentic generosity and selflessness required to embark on this journey with a loved one. See yourself for who you are – kindhearted and loyal, a caring advocate, a persevering warrior. No matter what the relationship is or has been, no matter how many times you feel impatient or even angry, this offering of yourself will, without a doubt, alter the course of what is likely the final stage of another's life. And in so doing, *you* may change forever. This was my experience and the experience of the many people I've interviewed and interacted with on this path.

I have lived through this experience twice, and on some levels I don't think it would be any easier if I did it ten more times. There were times when I felt so unbearably sad and alone that I could not see that there would be an end, a close to this chapter, and that there was life after loss. There were times when I thought that my grief would consume me and that I might never recover.

I am still recovering, almost two years after my mother's passing, but it's getting easier. These days I occasionally go an entire day without shedding a tear. And when the gremlins in my head start to tell me all the things I could have done differently, it is my work not to listen. I did my best and I know it.

I would be remiss if I did not share a simple idea with you that I hear myself saying over and over again in my work with clients -- that this is precious time with the person you care about so deeply. Care enough to be willing to jump in to help when she is at her most vulnerable, often at a great personal cost to you. So if you find yourself aggravated with the staff at the residence for things that are not life threatening, take a pause and ask yourself if putting out that "fire" is how you really want to spend your visiting time. And if your time is so limited that you feel like you have to multi-task during most of your visits, consider doing the logistical work through email or on the phone. Enlist another family member or hire a Care Manager to take some things off your plate.

Anything you can do to share the irreplaceable moments and simply be present will only serve to comfort and help you find peace when your loved one is gone.

And don't forget: taking caring of *you* is probably the most important thing you can do to sustain yourself. Ask for help, get respite, do things that you know will nourish you. Give yourself a break. Self soothe – have a massage, a walk in the woods, a day at the beach, meditate. Whatever it takes to give you some relief from the details of your loved one's needs. This is your oxygen mask.

GLOSSARY

Below is a list of some of the terms and acronyms you may encounter. If there is something you do not understand about any of these, or for that matter, anything at all related to your loved one's care, ask your doctor, a manager or nurse at the community, or call your local Ombudsmen office.

ADL Activities of Daily Living

AL or ALF Assisted Living Facility

CCRC Continuing Care Retirement Community

CCL Community Care Licensing

CSA Certified Senior Advisor

DNR Do Not Resuscitate

DPH Department of Public Health

DPOA Durable Power of Attorney

Hospice Care for seriously or terminally ill patients focused on comfort and emotional support, not curing (see box below)

Hoyer Lift A hydraulic lift used by caregivers to assist patients with limited mobility who need help transferring from bed to chair or walker and at other times

Long Term Care Ombudsmen Ombudsmen advocate and investigate complaints on behalf of residents living in a long -erm care facility

LTC Long-Term Care

Small Care Home/Board and Care Licensed assisted living, usually in a private home, with 4-10 residents

PCP Primary Care Provider

POLST Physician's Orders for Life Sustaining Treatment

Post Acute Care Also called "rehab" – usually a transitional stay between hospital and home or senior community

PRN medication Medication to be taken as needed, often for pain

RCFE Residential Care Facility for the Elderly

SNF Skilled Nursing Facility

A word about **Hospice**..... *People often assume that hospice should only be called when death is imminent. This is not necessarily so. Hospice, as part of a care plan, can provide physical comfort, emotional, and spiritual support for both the patient and the family, and can significantly improve the quality of life for the seriously or terminally ill and their family.*

Please do call your local hospice to learn more, even if you feel the time "hasn't come". It's always better to explore your options before a critical situation arises. It is not uncommon that a patient will go into hospice care, only to find a few months later that their change in condition is positive and that they no longer need this "comfort care". Hospice costs are usually covered by Medicare, Medicaid, and some other insurance providers. Check with your agent.

_____

_____

_____

_____

_____

_____

RESOURCES

Here is a partial list of places to look for help with insurance, medications, support groups, general topics on aging, caregiver support, etc. Even if your loved one lives in an assisted living facility, if you are responsible for decisions regarding their care, then you are a caregiver. Getting support is one of the best ways of taking care of yourself!

AARP
www.aarp.org

Assisted Living Directory
www.assisted-living-directory.com
Information on violations and citations in Assisted Living

Alzheimer's Association
www.alz.org

Benefits Check Up
www.benefitscheckup.org
Check here for benefits and assistance programs

Center for Medicare and Medicaid Services (CMS)
www.cms.org

ElderRoads
www.elderroads.com Elder Care Management, Family Coaching, Support Groups, Resources

Family Caregiver Alliance
www.caregiver.org

Leading Age
www.leadingage.org
Association of not-for-profit organizations
dedicated to a better aging experience

Long Term Care Ombudsmen
www.ltombdusmen.org
Advocacy for those living in long term care
environments, including assisted living and
skilled nursing facilities

Meals on Wheels
www.mowaa.org

Medicare
www.medicare.gov

Medicaid
www.medicaid.gov

National Council on Aging
www.NCOA.org

Needy Meds
www.needymeds.org
Free discount card to save up to 80% on
prescription and over-the-counter medications

ParaTransit
(google for local services in your area)
Low cost transportation for elderly or disabled individuals who cannot drive or use public transportation

Parkinson's Disease
www.apdaparkinson.org

Scan Foundation
www.thescanfoundation.org
Dedicated to aging with dignity, multiple resources for seniors, informational reports

Veterans Administration
www.va.gov
Check for availability of benefits for long term care needs for veterans

Please check my website, www.elderroads.com, for additional resources and articles of interest.

About the Author

Marcy Baskin is an Elder Care Manager, Family Coach, and Family Advocate practicing in northern California. She is a Certified Senior Advisor (CSA), a placement specialist, caregiver support group facilitator, a trained hospice volunteer, and a veteran of many elder care advocacy issues. She currently is on the faculty of the Health Navigation program at Sonoma State University, where she teaches Eldercare Management.

Since her mother's diagnosis and long decline with Alzheimer's disease, Marcy has devoted herself to supporting adult children who may be in the transitional relationship of "parenting their parent". She also works to support spouses and siblings of loved ones needing care due to a decline in physical and/or cognitive abilities.

When she isn't providing elder advocacy or holding support groups, Marcy spends her time practicing yoga (which she is sure helped to maintain her equanimity during the difficult years), writing, rescuing animals, cooking, and tending her organic vegetable garden. She lives in Sonoma County with her husband Steven, a grumpy Shi Tzu named KT and Nahla, an exuberant German Shepherd,

Please visit her website: www.elderroads.com

or email her at marcy@elderroads.com if you have questions about elder care issues of any kind.

"Things falling apart is a kind of testing and also a kind of healing. We think that the point is to pass the test or to overcome the problem, but the truth is that things don't really get solved. They come together and they fall apart. Then they come together again and fall apart again. It's just like that. The healing comes from letting there be room for all of this to happen: room for grief, for relief, for misery, for joy."

-Pema Chodron

CPSIA information can be obtained
at www.ICGtesting.com
Printed in the USA
LVOW01s1606240317
528386LV00007B/491/P